WORDPRESS USER'S MANUAL

HOW TO MANAGE THE CONTENT OF YOUR WEBSITE

VISUALWORKER.NET

Visualworker Editions

ISBN: 978-1-312-50350-2

@ 2014 Rodrigo Conceição dos Santos.

SUMMARY

This edition has been designed in order to help Visual Worker customers to manage the content of their pages using the CMS (content management system) Wordpress. It is based on the latest version to date of wordpress 3.6. First, you need access to the administrative area of your website, for this you must enter your admin address, for example:

http://yourwebsite.com/wp-admin/

C visualworker.net/wp-admin/

This address will be provided when you receive your access to the administrative area of your site. The page which will appear in returning one of these addresses will be this:

Enter your login / username and password / password then you must click on login name.

Username

Password

☐ Remember Me   Log In

Lost your password?

← Back to Click to Help

Once inside the wordpress interface, this page will appear:

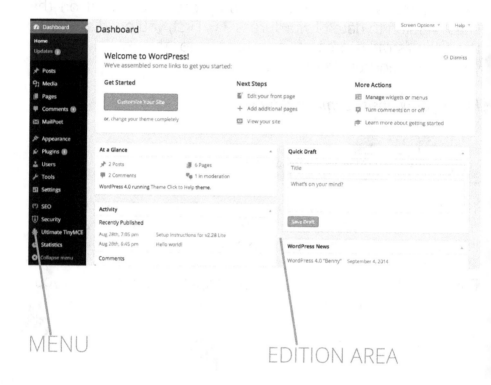

MENU

EDITION AREA

CHANGE LOGIN ACCESS

First of all we'll see how to change your login data. To do so, you have to pass your mouse by the word « user » in the menu, then another menu will be showed and you'll click on your profile.

On that page, you can change everything about your login data, password included.

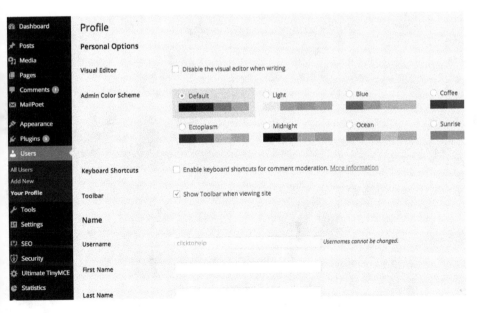

Mind clicking on the « update profil button », so you can be sure that you saved your changes. You'll see during this manual that the data changed have to be saved by clicking on many differents blue buttons of wordpress. If you don't, your changes won't be saved.

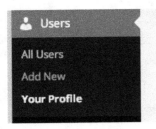

You can also add many others users to manage your website wordpress. These users can have different roles with restrictions, in order to have a better control.

To add new users, go to the tab "user" and click on the button "add new".

Then you'll be able to see a page where you'll have to write down your login data, Wordpress will tell you if your password is safe enough. If you want to have a safe password, use capital letters and numbers, with a minimum of 8 characters.

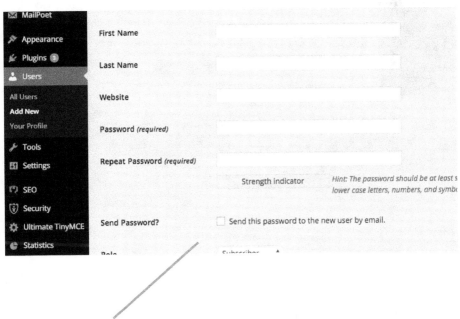

Don't forget to check *send password* so the new user will receive the password by mail.

You can see all your users on the tab user – all users/add author and user. To edit your user data you have to pass your mouse by your username and click on edit. Mind saving your changes.

CHANGE PAGE'S CONTENT

DIFFERENCE BETWEEN POSTS AND PAGES

Now we'll see how to change your wordpress site. You have two formats for your site, one of them is the post and the other is the page. The post: posts are used for pages inside the categories of your site.

Pages are normally used for permanent pages that don't have categories. For example, inside a menu like this the "service" tab sends you to the catergory and the pages that are found are posts.

On the other hand, pages like "contact" are permanent pages that will be edited on the tab pages inside the administrative zone wordpress.

Web Design et Graphisme - Genève

Services—
Website design
Cours Photoshop
Graphic Design
Portfolio+
Skills
Blog
Contact

CREATE A NEW POST

To create a post, click on the post tab inside the menu wordpress, then click on add a new post. On the page that will be showed you will be able to see different fields where you can change your wordpress site.

The first field is a title field. This one is the title of your page as it'll be showed in your website. The access link to that page will be created from this site. If you have a site with many languages, we'll be able to find a field for each language, but your link will be the one of the main language of your website. Inside the field that can be found above this one, you can add new information for you website, texts, images videos, everything.

You'll have a nice and advanced text editor, with the possibility of creating new lists, do texts justifications, you'll also have the choice about which typographie you want to use, the size of it and many other choices. The layout functions of your text will be listed on the end of this tutorial.

This visual layout can be found on the visual tab which is placed high at right of this field.

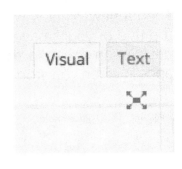

The visual layout editor of *Wordpress* looks like the one from the program *Word*. If you copy a text layouted on *Word,* the *Wordpress* editor will keep the layout.

You'll also have the choice for editing your text where you can place your html codes.

ADD A PICTURE

If you wish add new photos on your page, you'll have to click on the button add media. Click on this button and a new tab will be showed on this window. Then you need to click on "drop files/ select files", clicking on this button will allow you to choose the images that you can insert, these images have to be already in your computer.

Then a new window will be open. On that window, you can edit the title of your image, the link of that image, l'allignement, the description text and the "alt text" (this one is the text that will appear when you stop your mouse on the image.

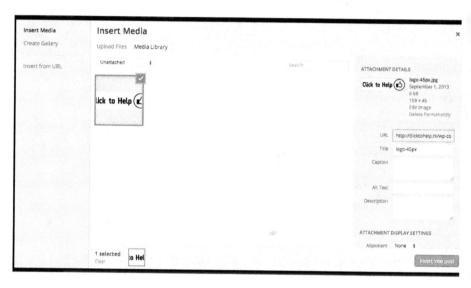

If your site has the function of image display on lightbox, you have to always put the link of the image towards mediafile if you want it to appear on lightbox.

If you want to add many images at once, choose them and click on insert into post. The images will appear where you were making the edition.

If you wish to erase a page, you have to click on this one and click on X.

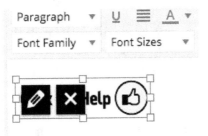

PUBLISH YOUR POST OR PAGE

Once your page is completely made you can get a preview by clicking on the preview button. A new window will appear showing the actual state of the edition.

Before posting that page, you have to choose one category on the category zone, if this one doesn't exist, you can create it by clicking on "add new category".

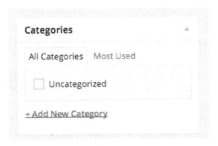

INCREASE YOUR SEO

EDIT THE TITLE AND THE DESCRIPTION OF YOUR PAGES

You can add many categories in the same post, this will make it appear on the correspondent tab of your site.

Before posting that page, mind rising your SEO, the edition zone can be found just under the edition field of your page.

WordPress SEO by Yoast

General   Page Analysis   Advanced   Social

Snippet Preview   (?)   **- Click to Help**
                         clicktohelp.tk//

Focus Keyword: (?)

SEO Title: (?)   - Click to Help

Meta Description: (?)

The meta description will be limited to 156 chars, chars left.

Meta Keywords:

If you type something above it will override your meta keywords template.

In that zone you'll be able to find the focus key word field, where you can insert one key word of your page. In the SEO title field, you can set the title of your page as it'll appear on google.

HOW TO BETTER WRITE YOUR TITLES FOR SEO

This title have to begin by words that are correspondent to your page, general data as the title of your company will come after this.

For example, if you want to set the price of a surgery in your office, you'll to put the word "price" before the word "Esthét plus". So you'll have to enter price – "Esthet plus". Inside the description zone, you insert the description of your site as you want it to be seen on google. Don't forget that these fields have a character limit.

Think about words that could be on a google search.

On the tab "meta key words", you can insert many key words for your website. This work will help you having a better ranking of your website on google searches. Once you have posted something, the SEO plug-in will show you a red, yellow or green mark that will tell you if the words are well choosen for your post or not. Once you've finished this work, you can post your page by clicking on the "Post" button.

MANAGE CATEGORIES AND POSTS

Your post will appear on the tab *post*, with all your *posts*.

EREASE A POST

On that page you'll find all pages that were posted in your website. To be able to edit them you have to pass by the post's name and click on edit. If you want to erase a post just click on "trash". If you want to erase something once for all, you have to go to the trash tab on this page and click on the word of the post that you have erased before, then click on "delete permanently".

	Title	A
	test	C

Edit | Quick Edit | Trash | View

	Title	Aut
	test	clicl

Restore | Delete Permanently

	Title	Aut

CREATE AND EDIT NEW PAGES

If you want to create permanent pages on the pages tab, you have to click on "add page". This procure is the same for posts, except for the fact that permanent pages don't belong to categories.

CREATE AND EDIT CATEGORIES

If you want to edit the categories that you have created, you have to go on the "post articles" tab -> categories, you can edit the name of these categories and create new ones.

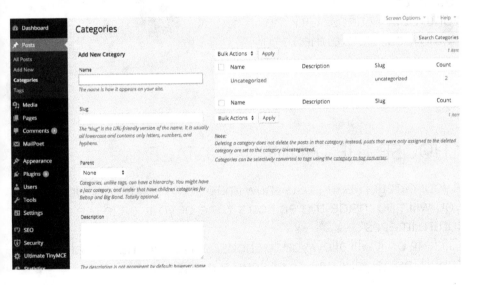

Mind saving your news by clicking on "apply" or "add new category".

EREASE A CATEGORY

You can also erase them by marking the categories you need to erase and going to the selection's tab that can be found above and under this zone bulk actions, click on it and choose delete, then apply.

CHOOSE THE THUMBNAIL IMAGE

If your categories or posts show images on mosaic in your website, you will find inside the edition's zone of your page the field "set future images".
Clicking on it will allow you to choose an image that can already be found inside your gallery or send a new one.

ADD CATEGORIES IN THE NAVIGATION MENU

To choose the pages and categories that will be showed on your website, you have to go on the appearance tab -> menu where you will be able to find different menus that are on your site.

Choose the menu that you want to edit in that zone on the right side then on the zone page at the bottom on the left side, then you have to mark the pages that you wish to add, after this, you'll need to click on "add to menu", they will appear on the right side of the page.

You can also change their orders by sliping then. Mind saving your changes by clicking on save menu.

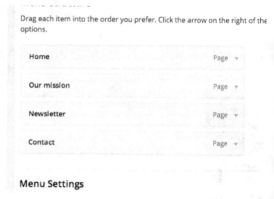

Menu Settings

EREASE CATEGORIES IN THE NAVIGATION MENU

If you want to erase one page of the menu, click on the name's page and a new zone will appear at the bottom then click on the red link "remove". Mind saving your changes by clicking on "save menu". This procedure is the same for adding categories, the categorie's zone can be found just above the page's zone.

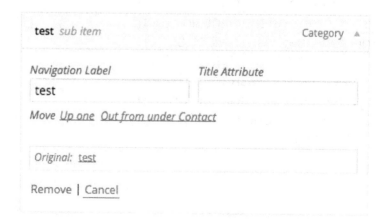

ADD LINKS TO THE NAVIGATION MENU

You can also add links to your navigation menu, you should go to the "custom links" area, enter the url address of the link and in the field "label" insert the title. Do not forget to click on "add to menu" then "save" menu.

MANAGE IMAGES AND COMMENTS

You can manage your gallery by going to media / library tab. A list of your images appear, the procedure to delete and edit is the same as for posts.

By clicking on the "edit" link, you can enter the texts belonging to the image SEO data to be better ranked on google images.

If your site has a comment function, they can be managed under the "comments" area.

CHANGE THE TITLE OF YOUR SITE

If you want to change the settings of your site, go to the "setting - general" tab where you can change the title of your site.

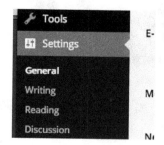

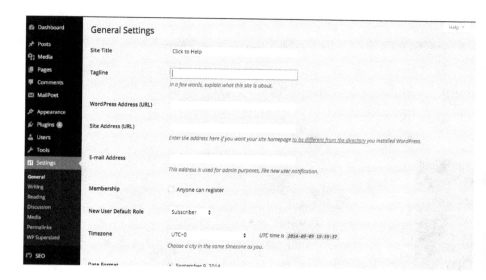

To change the home page of your site, go to "setting – reading", choose one of the pages already published on your site as the home page. On media setting, you can change the standard image sizes.

DIFFERENT FUNCTIONS, DIFFERENT PLUGINS

EDIT LANGUAGES OF YOUR SITE

Multilanguage - qTranslate

If you have a multilanguage website, you can add/erase any languages on your website. To do so, you need to go in "setting languages", on the first field you can choose the main language.

In the zone at the bottom on the right side, you can activate and deactivate any language.

Flag	Nom	Action		
	Deutsch	Activer	Editer	Supprimer
	中文	Activer	Editer	Supprimer
	suomi	Activer	Editer	Supprimer
	Nederlands	Activer	Editer	Supprimer
	Svenska	Activer	Editer	Supprimer
	Italiano	Activer	Editer	Supprimer
	Română	Activer	Editer	Supprimer
	Magyar	Activer	Editer	Supprimer
	日本語	Activer	Editer	Supprimer
	Español	Activer	Editer	Supprimer
	Tiếng Việt	Activer	Editer	Supprimer
	العربية	Activer	Editer	Supprimer
	Português	Activer	Editer	Supprimer
	Polski	Activer	Editer	Supprimer
	galego	Activer	Editer	Supprimer
	EN	Désactiver	Editer	Supprimer
	FR	Désactiver	Editer	Défaut
Flag	Nom	Action		

Slideshows with Portfolio slideshow

If you have the function of making new slideshows on your website, you can add new ones to your page. To do so, go to the edition's zone of your post/page, at the bottom you can find a portfolio zone slideshow.

First of all, click on "upload" and "manage images", choose the images you wish to insert, don't forget: your images need to have the same size.

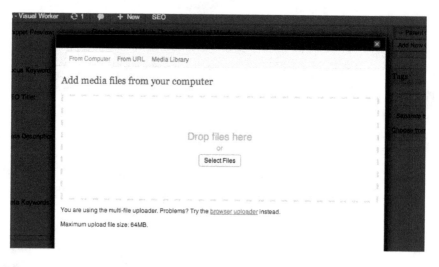

Once your images are sent, click on "save changes" and close the window.

Then, at the top of the page, click on the zone "publish" and "save draft".

Then, go to the bottom of the page again, on the portfolio's tab slideshow and copy the line of the code that can be found between the hooks.

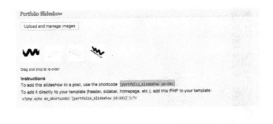

Insert this line on the page where you want it to be showed in your slideshow.

Post the page, the slideshow will appear on your website page.

If you wish to change images of your slideshow, go to the bottom on green, the portfolio's zone slideshow and click on "update and manage photos", then a new window will show up.

Click on the "gallery" tab to erase images, click on the link show that corresponds to the image that can be found on the right side of the list.

In the edition's zone of images, click on "delete".

Finally, don't forget to click on the link "save all changes" to make sure that everything will be updated.

Advanced layout edition - tinyMCE

In the editing area of your posts and pages you will find tools to advanced layout. These tools work as in most text editors.

Some tools are specific to the web, here are their functions:

Br to make the jumps to line

You Tube to add youtube videos on your page

allows you to create tables, you set the columns and rows.

For your paragraph appears as you want, you should always select it and click one of the alignment buttons.

This may have no visual impact in the editor but the html code it will change.

WORDPRESS APPLICATION

You can update text and images on your site from your mobile phone or tablet with the WordPress application. We will see the Android and iPhone versions, the application is almost the same on other systems.

ADD YOUR SITE TO YOUR APP

The Wordpress app gives you the ability to edit (and create new) your posts / articles and your pages, you will be able to change the text and images. Several functions are not available in the application.

The first step to do is download the application (for iPhone in the App Store, Android Google Play and so on).
Once you download the app and open the installation window opens, click the "add self-hosted Wordpress blog" option / Add a self-hosted blog.

IPHONE   ANDROID

Then add the details of your site:
URL: The URL of your site | Username: Your login for your website |
Password: your password

IPHONE   ANDROID

EDIT A POST

If you want to edit a post, click on posts, to edit a page click on "pages", editing will be done the same way for both.

IPHONE   ANDROID

Press the post / page you want to edit or create a new building on the icon:

In the android version after choosing the post you must press the edit icon:

IPHONE   ANDROID

The editing window opens, simply fill or modify the fields, if you wish to insert photos or videos press icons:

Do not forget to click publish or update at the end.

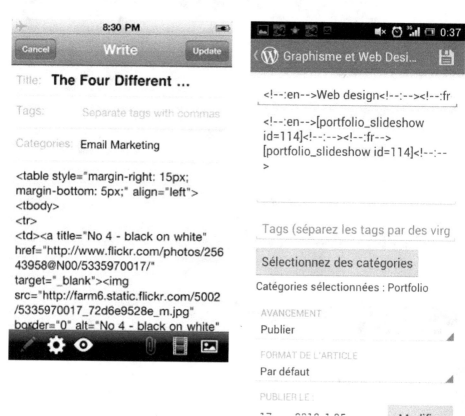